D0914307

Lebanon A to Z

A MIDDLE EASTERN MOSAIC

Marijean Boueri, Jill Boutros, Joanne Sayad

illustrations by Tatiana Sabbagh

ACKNOWLEDGEMENTS

Many generous people offered their time and expertise in making *Lebanon A to Z: A Middle Eastern Mosaic* accurate and infinitely richer. We would like to thank our friend Julie Hannouche as well as PublishingWorks' Jeremy Townsend for their patience and professional guidance; historian and author Nina Jidejian; Dr. Helen Sader; Fifi Abdelnour; American Community School faculty Charlene Mikdashi, Barea Gawhary, Rula Kahil, Barbara Bashour and Sarah Reaburn; Dr. Leila Badre, curator of the American University of Beirut's Archeological Museum, and the Children's Program Committee: Claude Issa, Alexa Hechaime, Amal Rababy and Rhonda Trad. Finally, thanks to Jamale Boutros, Tsaka Jichi, Betty Karam, Terry Kassab, Dr. Barbara Katsos, Esq., Dolly Khairallah, Nada Melki, Nabil Najjar, and Nancy Rayess for contributing a panache of eclectic tidbits.

Library of Congress Cataloguing-in-Publication Data
Lebanon A to Z: A Middle Eastern Mosaic / Marijean Boueri, Jill Boutros, Joanne Sayad.
Illustrated by Tatiana Sabbagh p. cm.
ISBN 0-9744803-4-7
Includes index.
1. Lebanon - Juvenile literature.
Boueri, Marijean. I. Boutros, Jill. II. Sayad, Joanne. III.
Title. DS80.B68 2005

Book design by Nidal Achkar Bou Abdallah and Sally Reed.

Anis Commercial Printing Press, Beirut, Lebanon
First Edition 2005

PublishingWorks
4 Franklin street
Exeter, New Hampshire 03833

www.lebanonatoz.com

To Naji and our four - your support inspires me. Also to the
spirit of cooperation and hard work, and the friendships
made along the way - again, priceless.
J.B.

For Kevin, Patrick and Grace
RAFYM
M.M.B.

In memory of my mother and grandmother
Heartfelt thanks to Dr. Edward and Marie Sayad
Especially for Ralph, Ralph junior, Jamie and Christopher
J.K.S.

To Bassam
who helped me discover and understand Lebanon
T.B.S.

Table of Contents

Look for my Phoenician friend on every page. He has lots of fun facts to share.

Words in bold face are defined in the glossary.

Foreign words are *italicized*.

Marhaba! *Salut*! Hello!

My name is Kareem and I am very happy to introduce you to my country, Lebanon. From the time I was born, eleven years ago, my family has lived in Beirut, the capital city. My sister, Amal, and I attend a French school not far from our home. In school we study three languages—Arabic, French and English. At home we speak a combination of all three.

There is so much to show you!
With the alphabet as our guide,
let's explore Lebanon.

Ahlan wa sahlan!
Bienvenue!
Welcome!

Alphabet

Imagine life without the ABCs! A very important contribution from Lebanon to the world is the alphabet.

Before the alphabet, people expressed their ideas with hieroglyphs (picture symbols) and cuneiform (wedge symbols). Hieroglyphs were so hard to learn that only a few specially trained people called scribes knew how to write them.

Lebanon's early settlers, the **Phoenicians**, were clever traders. About 3000 years ago, they developed a new script of 22 symbols to represent the sounds of their language. As they sailed back and forth across the Mediterranean Sea, they shared this new alphabet with others. The Phoenician alphabet made it possible for many more people to read and write. I'm glad my **ancestors** gave the world a better way to communicate.

Phonics, the study of sound and symbol, comes from the word Phoenician.

Many European alphabets were developed from the Phoenician script.

Beirut

Bustling and busy, Beirut is home to more than half of the Lebanese population. Ancient and modern mingle on every street in this city of contrasts.

Walking to school, we see *Sitt* (Madame) Nour lowering a basket from her balcony to collect the groceries delivered by the neighborhood vendor. Just next to her home is a sleek modern office building, headquarters of a large international company. A long, black sedan slows to avoid the street merchant pushing his wooden cart filled with colorful fruits and vegetables. Across the street, a female jogger wearing a t-shirt and shorts passes a veiled woman on her way to the market. Contrasts like these make Beirut a dynamic and interesting city.

Beirut is legendary for having been destroyed and rebuilt many times. History books tell of destruction by tidal wave, earthquake, fire and war!

5

Cedars

During a recent school trip to the ancient cedar forest in northern Lebanon, some friends and I carried out an experiment. We wanted to find out how many of us it would take to encircle one of the oldest cedar trees. Holding hands, we embraced the tree. How many of us do you think we needed? Five? Seven? No! It took twelve classmates to reach around its trunk. Our guide estimated that tree to be more than 1500 years old! The majestic cedars of Lebanon are among the earth's oldest living plants.

Lebanese cedars used to cover the mountains from north to south, but thousands of years of cutting trees without replanting have stripped away all but a few of the oldest trees. A conservation project has seen a million young trees replanted, but the slow-growing cedar needs hundreds of years to mature.

Our class promised to become caretakers of the land. Lebanon's environment depends on it.

TREE OF TRAVELS
Phoenician, Egyptian, Greek and Roman sailors navigated the seas with boats made of sturdy cedar, an ideal wood for shipbuilding because it provided long shafts for masts and did not decay.

TREE OF THE AFTERLIFE Egyptians used cedar **resin** as an ingredient in mummy-making.

TREE OF GOD King Solomon's temple was built with prized Lebanese cedar wood, as were the mosques of Morocco and Spain.

Diversity

Lebanon is home to people of many different backgrounds. Such **diversity** of religious and ethnic groups creates a rich mosaic unique to the Middle East. Eighteen religious communities are officially recognized in Lebanon. Let me introduce you to some of my friends.

My name is Fadia. I am Druze. My village is in the beautiful Chouf Mountains. I do not know much about my religion. It is kept secret and shared only among the elders. I do know that our wisdom comes from many sources, including the Bible, the Koran, Greek philosophy and Far Eastern beliefs. Many Druze wear traditional Lebanese clothing. Although we are small in number throughout the world, we are very important in Lebanon. We keep many mountain traditions alive. I hope to learn more about my heritage when I am older.

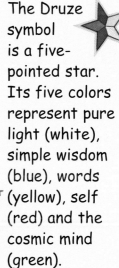

The Druze symbol is a five-pointed star. Its five colors represent pure light (white), simple wisdom (blue), words (yellow), self (red) and the cosmic mind (green).

Bonjour! My name is Maroun. I am named after Saint Maron, the founder of the Maronite Church. His feast day, February 9, is a national holiday in Lebanon. The Maronites are under the spiritual leadership of the Pope in Vatican City. My family and I go to church on Sundays where I enjoy singing in the choir. Happy or sad, the songs stay with me all day long. Next weekend our family will celebrate the baptism of my new cousin, Charbel. We will gather to welcome the baby into the church community just as they did for me nine years ago.

Syriac is the closest language to Aramaic, the language spoken by Jesus. Parts of the Maronite liturgy are celebrated in Syriac.

The Vatican has canonized saints from Lebanon: St. Charbel, St. Rafqa and St. Hardini.

Ahlan! My name is Alia. I'm a Shi'ite Moslem. We live in a village which rests on the rocky cliffs above Tyre. My father has a special job in our village. He is the *mue'zzin*. Five times a day, he enters the mosque and climbs to the top of the **minaret** to recite the call to prayer. Everyone in the village knows him. I am studying hard at school because someday I would like to be a doctor. I am also learning to recite the Koran, our holy book, like my parents. Every year, on the day of *Ashoura*, we mourn the death of Hussein, grandson of the prophet, whom Shi'ites believe to be the rightful successor to Mohammad.

Islam in Arabic means "surrender, submission, commitment and peace."

13

Hi! I am Roula and I'm Greek Orthodox. My family lives in Achrafieh, a hilly part of Beirut known for its beautiful architecture. Fifty days prior to Easter, I begin a fast. I will not eat meat or animal products like cheese and eggs during this time, and the adults in my family will not eat or drink until noon each day. In this way we remember Christ's sacrifice for us. On Palm Sunday, *Shaanineh*, I wear my best dress. At church that day, the children carry long candles decorated with flowers and ribbons. We parade through the neighborhood, following the priest in procession. The next week is Easter, our biggest celebration of the year. *Christos Anesti*!

During the 19th century, when Beirut was a small walled city, the keys to its seven gates were entrusted to members of seven Greek Orthodox families. In the early morning the gates were opened, then closed and locked again at nightfall.

Marhaba! I am Walid, a Sunni Moslem. Moslems believe that God's word was revealed to the prophet Mohammad. Next year, when I turn twelve, I will fast during the month of **Ramadan**. This means I won't eat from sunrise until sunset. Every evening at sunset our family will gather for a special meal called *Iftar*. During Ramadan we share money and food with the poor. Ramadan ends with a three-day celebration called *Eid el-Fitr*, the Breaking of the Fast.

Lailat al Qadr, or Night of Power, is celebrated the evening of the 27th day of Ramadan. It commemorates the night the prophet Mohammad received the first revelation from God.

17

Parev! My name is Hagop. I live in Anjar, a town in the Bekaa Valley which was built many years ago especially for the Armenian people. Armenians have become an important part of Lebanon's cultural patchwork. Because we follow the old Christian calendar, we celebrate Christmas on January 6, the **Epiphany**. I study Armenian as well as Arabic, French and English, so I use three alphabets and speak four languages! On Saturdays, I join other Armenian children to learn traditional dances and songs at the community center. Afterwards, we eat a spicy sausage called *soujouk*.

Excavations around Anjar in 1947 uncovered a walled city of the Omayyad caliphs with a palace, mosque, shops and *hammams* (oriental baths).

I love you when you
bow in your mosque,
kneel in your temple,
pray in your church.

For you and I
are sons of one religion,
and it is the spirit.

Khalil Gibran,
The Voice of the Poet

Entertainment

The latest movies from around the world play in Lebanon's cinemas, but our culture distinguishes itself through oriental music and dance.

The *dabké* is Lebanon's national dance. **Folkloric** performers from across the country dance the *dabké*, wearing colorful, traditional costumes. Holding hands and moving in a semi-circle, dancers tell a romantic or sentimental story of village life. The steps are easy to learn, so toddlers and grandparents can enjoy the dance together.

"A great singer is he who sings our silences." Khalil Gibran

No singer represents Lebanon better than Fairuz. Her songs of love and patriotism have a special place in the hearts of Lebanese people around the world. My parents tell us how her voice gave them courage and hope during the sad days of the war. They speak of an unforgettable concert set amidst the ruins of war-torn Beirut, when Fairuz sang to the people encouraging them to "stand up" and stand together.

The Al-Bustan, Baalbek, Beiteddine and Byblos music festivals host international and regional stars.

Teta & Jiddo

Jiddo & Teta

Khali & Mart Khali

Mama & Baba

Amti & Joz Amti

Ibn Amti

Ibn Khali & Bint Khali

Karim & Amal

Bint Amti

Family

Lebanese families have strong, deep roots. In our family, my grandparents live in the apartment downstairs, and my aunt and her family live upstairs. Amal and I always have someone to care for us when my parents are at work. The housekeeper is there when we get home from school. *Teta*, our grandmother, gives us lunch and stays to check our homework. We play with our cousins almost every afternoon.

Look closely at the family tree. I have different names for my uncles and cousins. Arabic has many more words than English or French to describe family members.

Grandma: Teta
Grandpa: Jiddo

Mother: Mama
Father: Baba

Husband: Joz
Wife: Mart

MOTHER'S SIDE

Uncle: Khali
Aunt: Khalti
Cousin (Uncle's son):
Ibn Khali
Cousin (Aunt's son):
Ibn Khalti
Cousin (Uncle's daughter):
Bint Khali
Cousin (Aunt's daughter):
Bint Khalti

FATHER'S SIDE

Uncle: Ammi
Aunt: Amti
Cousin (Uncle's son):
Ibn Ammi
Cousin (Aunt's son):
Ibn Amti
Cousin (Uncle's daughter):
Bint Ammi
Cousin (Aunt's daughter):
Bint Amti

Parents are sometimes called by the name of their firstborn son. *Abu* Ramzi, for example, means the father of Ramzi. *Imm* Ramzi is his mother.

Gibran

"Generosity is giving more than you can, and pride is taking less than you need."

"The truly great man is he who would master no one, and who would be mastered by none."

The Lebanese admire the poetry and art of Khalil Gibran (1883–1931).

Gibran grew up as the second of four children in Bcharré, a mountain village in northern Lebanon. As a child, he traveled to Boston, Massachusetts, when his parents **emigrated** to escape **famine**, but Gibran never forgot his Lebanese roots.

His masterpiece, *The Prophet*, tells of a man coming down from the mountains preparing to sail away forever from the shores of his homeland. The man speaks to the people who gather to say goodbye, offering words of wisdom on many important subjects such as love, children, joy and sorrow, and freedom.

The Khalil Gibran museum in Bcharré displays his artwork and writings.

Khalil Gibran's wisdom still speaks to people around the world. Since it was first published in 1923, *The Prophet* has been translated into more than 20 languages, and read by millions of people. In 1961, as John F. Kennedy gave his **inaugural** address, he immortalized Gibran's words when he said: "Ask not what your country can do for you; ask what you can do for your country."

A statue honoring Gibran has been erected in Boston.

Home

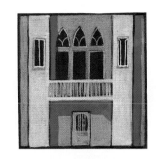

Ask a Lebanese person, "Where are you from?" and it is likely you will get two answers, both of them true. Though most people in Lebanon make their homes in city centers such as Tripoli and Beirut, almost everyone identifies with an ancestral village. This is another example of how traditional and modern life blend in Lebanon.

Our family lives in a busy shopping district in Beirut called Hamra. My grandparents own the building we live in, and gave each of their children an apartment. City sounds are the background music of our days. In the late afternoons we hear the call to prayer while church bells ring, taxi cabs honk and peddlers announce their wares.

Weekends, holidays, and all summer long we leave city life behind. We have a second home with my mother's parents, who live in their mountain village. Our home in the village is very different from our city apartment. The old stone house with a red-tiled roof sits in the middle of a huge garden. In the arched *qabu* under the house, we play *cache-cache*, hiding among the large terracotta jars of preserves stored there for the winter. Days are spent outside playing with our friends. Whenever there is no school, this is where we love to be.

People can often tell which village you are from by your last name.

29

Inscriptions

Lebanon's history is literally carved in stone. Just a few miles north of Beirut at *Nahr el Kelb* (Dog River), every conquering army or colonizer since Pharaoh Ramses II has left a permanent mark of its presence. Seventeen inscriptions line the river gorge at its entrance to the sea.

These inscriptions, called *stelae*, are written in the invader's native script. The oldest carving is Egyptian hieroglyphs, followed by Babylonian cuneiform, Greek, Latin and Arabic inscriptions. The most recent plaques were left by French and British troops in the early twentieth century.

An epigraphist is a person who studies ancient inscriptions. Their work helps **archeologists** and historians to better understand past civilizations.

CONQUERORS WHO LEFT THEIR MARK AT THE DOG RIVER

RAMSES II (thirteenth century BC)
Became Pharaoh at age 10! Famous for building many temples and monuments. He reigned for 67 years.

NEBUCHADNAZZAR II (sixth century BC) Babylonian king famous for constructing the Hanging Gardens of Babylon, one of the Seven Wonders of the Ancient World.

ALEXANDER THE GREAT (fourth century BC)
Alexander the Great was privileged to have Aristotle, the great Greek philosopher, as his tutor. He became king at age 20, forced the Greeks to unify, and went on to spread Greek culture in Asia through conquest.

MARCUS AURELIUS (second century AD)
One of Rome's "good" emperors, Marcus Aurelius was an excellent military leader who surprisingly kept a thoughtful journal he called *Meditations*. His insights still have meaning for us today : "What is not good for the swarm is not good for the bee." "Remember this–that very little is needed to make a happy life."

Jeita

Drip. Drop. Drip. Drop.

The steady beat of water drops is the only sound that breaks the deep silence inside the tunnel leading to the enormous caves of Jeita Grotto. Inside the caves we enter a mammoth new world with thousands of geological formations called **stalagmites** and **stalactites**. Limestone dripping for millions of years has created a natural landscape of underground sculptures. My father compares them to indoor icicles, but I think the formations are so strange that this must be what another planet looks like. Imagine how the first explorers felt!

In 1836, an American man hunting in the valley discovered a mysterious, watery cave. Firing a shot into the darkness he tried to gauge the size of the cave; no echo was heard. The cave was enormous!

More than a century later, **spelunkers** explored a second cave at the site, this one farther up the mountainside and dry as dust. The two caves are connected inside, and reach almost 6 kilometers (3.6 miles) into the mountain. Today, visitors can see them both: the upper cave on foot, and the lower one by boat.

The longest stalactite in the world is found in Jeita Grotto. It is more than 8 meters (23 feet) long!

An easy way to remember the difference between a stalactite and a stalagmite is the stalactite has a "c" in it for ceiling. Stalagmite has a "g" for ground.

Kaak

Before sunrise, Abu Ayad fills his bicycle cart with fresh, hot *kaak* from the local bakery. Crusty, chewy and covered with sesame seeds–similar to a soft pretzel or bagel–*kaak* is one of Lebanon's favorite street foods. Vendors such as Abu Ayad sell this purse-shaped bread in neighborhoods across Beirut, stuffing it with *zaatar* (locally grown wild thyme), *sumac* (a lemony spice), or spreadable cheese.

In my neighborhood, Abu Ayad jingles his bicycle bell, calling out, *"Kaak! Kaak!"* just after I arrive home from school. He waits, knowing Amal and I will rush downstairs, money in hand. Her choice will be cheese, and mine *zaatar*.

Lebanese people like to eat *zaatar* in the morning. They say it "opens the brain cells" and makes you smarter!

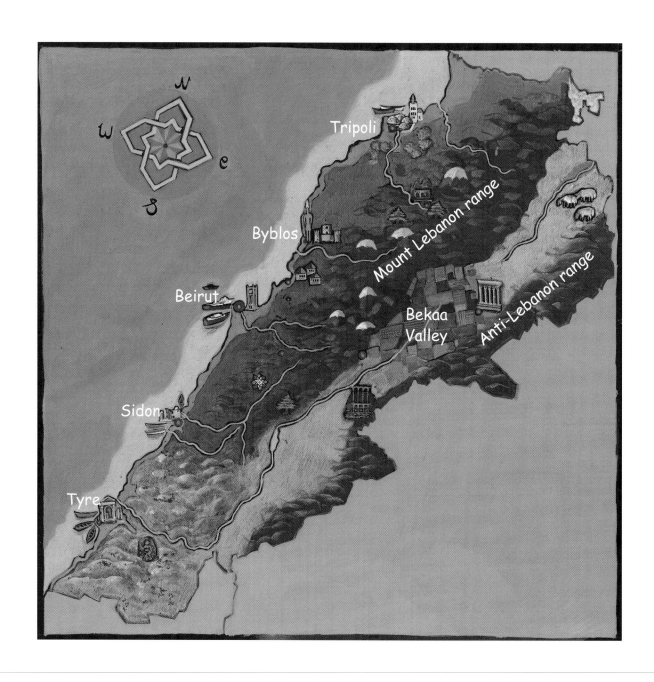

Lebanon

One of the world's smallest countries, Lebanon boasts amazing diversity of geography, climate, population and language.

GEOGRAPHY

The Coastal Plain is home to cities inhabited for thousands of years.

The Mount Lebanon range has majestic, snow-covered peaks that rise 3000 meters above sea level.

The Bekaa Valley is surprisingly flat, fertile farmland, home to many ancient cities.

The Anti-Lebanon range forms a natural border with Syria.

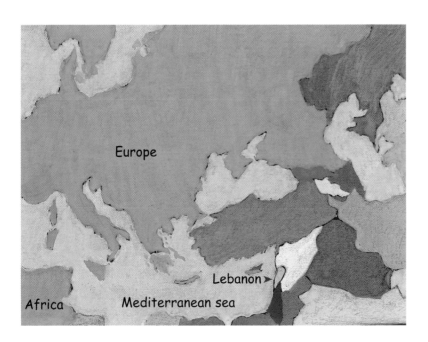

Lebanon is the only Middle Eastern country that doesn't have a desert.

The largest pine forest in the Middle East is near Jezzine, Lebanon.

CLIMATE

Spring thaws enrich the soil and color the mountains with wildflowers.

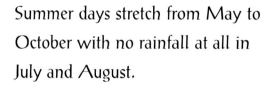

Summer days stretch from May to October with no rainfall at all in July and August.

Autumn harvests yield olives, grapes, apples, and figs in abundance.

Winter snow allows for cold-weather sports such as skiing and snowboarding.

POPULATION

Estimated at 4 million. Lebanese descend from many peoples, including Canaanites, Phoenicians, Assyrians, Arabs, and Turks.

LANGUAGE

Arabic is the official national language. French and English are spoken as well. Road signs appear in all three languages.

GOVERNMENT

Lebanon is a republic. On November 22, 1943, it achieved its independence from the French mandate. Traditionally, the president of Lebanon is a Maronite Christian, the Prime Minister, a Sunni Moslem, and the Speaker of the Parliament, a Shi'ite.

MONEY

LL Lebanese lira are printed in Arabic and French.
$ American dollars are also widely used.

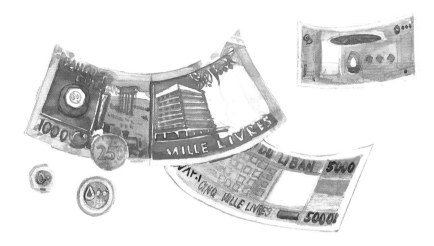

 The first silver coins were minted in Tyre during the 5th century BC.

Today's Lebanon was part of the Ottoman Empire for 400 years (1517-1917).

Arabic is read from right to left, except for numbers, which are read from left to right!

39

Mezza

"Tfaddalo!"

Jiddo (grandfather) and *Teta* (grandmother) invite everyone to begin Sunday lunch at a restaurant along the Berdowni River in Zahlé. Aunts, uncles and cousins pull up their chairs to an extra long table decorated with an oversized platter of garden-fresh vegetables. The table is laden with *mezza*, which means "little portions." Terracotta bowls filled with salads, dips and savory pies zigzag across the table. A woman from the village prepares the warm shepherd's bread that we use for dipping and eating.

Time passes as we talk, laugh and refill our plates. Some adults sip *arak*, an anise-flavored drink. Smoke from my uncle's apple-scented *arguileh* perfumes the air. By the time the main course arrives, we are stuffed!

For dessert, we move to another table to enjoy fresh fruit and Arabic sweets. The meal ends with tiny cups of cardamom-flavored coffee.

Green, fresh parsley is the main ingredient of *tabbouleh*, Lebanon's national salad.

43

Nai

My mother is a musician.

Though she plays many instruments, her specialty is the *nai*. The *nai* has been used in classical Arabic music for nearly 4,500 years. Traditionally, shepherds played it to their flocks for its peaceful, soothing sound.

The *nai* resembles a recorder. It is a reed instrument, which means the musician blows across a mouthpiece made of reed to create sound. Mother tells us it is one of the most difficult wind instruments to learn. Six fingers cover the holes on the top side of the *nai*, and the thumb seals the one hole underneath. As her fingers move, the notes change.

Once a month, my mother practises with a group of musicians who play classical oriental instruments. One man brings his *oud*, which is similar to a guitar. Another friend plays the *qanun*, or lap harp. The third keeps time with the *derbakké*, a drum shaped like an hour glass. Amal and I join in playing the tambourine, which in Arabic is called the *daff*. The room vibrates to the beat of the music.

Lebanon has a National Symphony Orchestra which performs both European classical and Oriental Arabic music.

45

Olives

One weekend every November, we drive north to Koura to help with a friend's olive harvest. Since the picking is done by hand, each of us has an important role to play.

Starting from the top of the ladder, I pick hundreds of olives as I move slowly down the tree. When the basket fills, another helper carries it away to the stone olive press, called a *makbass*. The pressed olives make a paste, which is then forced through a type of felt to separate the solids from the liquids.

As a reward for our hard day's work, we take home glass jars of "liquid gold." Our healthy Mediterranean diet is based on olive oil. My mom will use it in cooking and preserving all year long.

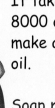

It takes about 8000 olives to make a gallon of oil.

Soap made from olive oil is great for hair, skin and even the laundry!

Phoenicians

History remembers our Phoenician ancestors as traders, sailors and makers of the famous murex purple dye, which was extracted from the shell of a sea snail.

Around 3000 years ago, trade took the Phoenicians all across the Mediterranean Sea in their sturdy cedarwood ships. The Phoenicians' unsurpassed knowledge of winds, tides and navigation by stars enabled their sailors to reach ports in Great Britain and around the Horn of Africa. They traded precious textiles, glass and metalwork made in Phoenicia.

The four major Phoenician cities still exist as Lebanon's largest and most populated urban centers. Tyre, Byblos, and Sidon were followed in importance by Beirut. Every Phoenician city had its own king, gods and goddesses. Each acted independently in trade and defense against invasion.

The Phoenicians kept most of their records on papyrus, a paper made of reeds. Unfortunately, papyrus disintegrates over time. As a result, most of what historians know of the Phoenicians comes from records kept by other civilizations.

Scientists estimate that it took more than 30,000 murex shells to make just 250 grams (half a pound) of the precious purple dye.

Wearing purple was the exclusive right of royalty. During the Middle Ages, it was illegal for a commoner to wear purple.

Qadisha Valley

No place in Lebanon rivals the natural beauty of the Qadisha Valley. Stretching 50 kilometers (31 miles) from Lebanon's highest mountain down to the sea, the Qadisha Valley is a hiker's paradise. An ambitious trek might include scaling sheer cliffs, exploring a multitude of caves, and photographing cascading waterfalls. You may choose to visit one of the seven monasteries that dot the trail up the gorge. At the summit, the ancient cedar forest awaits.

"Qadisha" means "holy" in the ancient Syriac language. For hundreds of years the Qadisha Valley has been known as a special place. Breathtaking natural beauty and religious tradition make the Qadisha Valley magnificent.

The Qadisha Valley is one of only a few places in the world registered on UNESCO's World Heritage list under the category of "cultural landscapes." A cultural landscape is a place where people and the natural environment form a special relationship.

Ruins

My cousins from Australia visited during the summer. They were most impressed by the layers of history we explored in Lebanon's major archaeological sites.

We took them first to Baalbek, the ancient Roman "City of the Sun." Today's engineers can only wonder at the skill shown by the architects and craftsmen who created this marvel. Stones larger than a school bus were cut from a local quarry, moved to the site, and nestled together so tightly that even today not a single sheet of paper can slip between them. Pillars seven stories tall framed the Temple of Jupiter–the largest in all the Roman Empire. Built over the course of centuries, the ruins at Baalbek remain as impressive as ever.

Byblos is one of the oldest continuously inhabited cities in the world. People have lived in this port town for 7000 years. During the Chalcolithic Age (3500-3100 BC), when people worked with bronze and stone, one custom was to bury the dead in large clay jars. Men were buried with their weaponry and women with their jewelry. Food and water were put in the jars to provide nourishment for the journey to the afterlife. About 1500 burial jars have been unearthed to date.

The ruins at Tyre give us an inkling of the city's wealth and power in ancient days. Prosperous and proud, the Tyrians believed they could resist even Alexander the Great's conquering army. Indeed, capturing Tyre proved to be one of Alexander's most difficult battles. It took his soldiers seven months to build a causeway connecting the mainland to the island fortress where the citizens had taken refuge. In the end, the defeated Tyrian people were either killed or enslaved. Over time the causeway disappeared as silt and sand changed the landscape.

While exploring Tyre, we saw the remnants of a complete Roman city including the baths, **aqueduct**, **necropolis** and **agora**. Large sections of an enormous Roman hippodrome built to accommodate 30,000 spectators still stand today. Sitting on the bleachers, one can imagine the chariots charging around the track. Some games were held in a unique water-filled arena. The ruins look especially beautiful at sunset.

The word Byblos comes from the Greek word, βιβλοσ, for book.

Sports

Lebanon's ideal climate makes it a great place to enjoy outdoor sports all year long. Most days, my friends and I organize a game of *football* (soccer) or *basket* (basketball) during recess. In Boy Scouts, we hike and camp year round, discovering Lebanon's wilderness. After we finish our homework, Amal and I rollerblade or scooter on the Corniche, a wide sidewalk lined with palm trees along the sea.

From May to October we swim and spend time at the beach. During the winter months, many people head to the mountains to play in the snow. The nearest ski resorts are less than an hour's drive from Beirut.

During the month of April, it is possible to snow ski in the morning and water ski after lunch.

Lebanese athletes brought home medals from the Olympic Games in 1952, 1972 and 1980.

Tawleh

In French, it's *tric-trac*. In English, it's backgammon. But by any name, *tawleh* is a very popular Lebanese pastime.

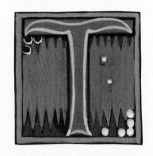

I walk with my *jiddo* (grandfather) to the local *ah'way* (traditional café) where his friends gather with their boards in the late afternoon. Two by two, they challenge each other as I stand aside to watch and learn.

This fast-paced game of strategy and luck has opponents racing around the board, rolling dice and positioning their discs to be the first to reach "home."

Today's game has changed very little since its origin 5000 years ago. During the Middle Ages, however, the *tawleh* board took on a new shape. Church officials tried to outlaw playing *tawleh* because they believed it distracted the public from praying. Craftsmen disguised the boards by folding them in half to hide the playing surface inside. Today's boards remain folded, and are now decorated with inlaid mother of pearl geometric designs which make them beautiful keepsakes.

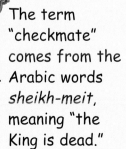

Tawleh is the oldest known board game—even older than chess!

The term "checkmate" comes from the Arabic words *sheikh-meit*, meaning "the King is dead."

University

Homework, homework, homework! Sometimes we feel that is all we do. Lebanon is renowned for its fine yet rigorous educational system. At fourteen, all students must pass the Lebanese *Brevet*, a national exam. Three years later, during the final year of high school, students spend several months preparing for the Lebanese and French *Baccalaureate* exams. Those who pass can skip the freshman year of university and enter as sophomores.

When the time comes for me to make a decision about university, I will choose from more than twenty colleges and universities in Lebanon which offer programs in Arabic, French, or English.

The American University of Beirut is one of the oldest and most prestigious of all. Its verdant hillside campus in the heart of Beirut, with an underground tunnel leading to its own beach, attracts students from dozens of countries around the world. *L'Université Saint Joseph*, the first French university in the region, was established in 1860. The Lebanese University, with campuses across the country, is the only public university.

No matter which system I choose, university education in Lebanon offers a solid foundation for my future.

The Roman empire's most prestigious law school was located in *Berytus* (Beirut). The teachings of Gaius (a famous law professor) are still the foundations of Western law practice.

61

Vineyards

Of all the crops grown in Lebanon, grapes are perhaps the most popular. Some are grown especially for eating, and others just for making wine. Grapevines blanket the fertile Bekaa Valley and stretch across terraces built into the mountainsides. Most homes outside the city train a vine to reach up and cover a sunny terrace, providing fruit and a shady "ceiling" at the same time.

Grapes and winemaking have been important to this part of the world for thousands of years. Phoenician merchants exported rich, sweet wines in clay jars, called *amphorae*, to port cities around the Mediterranean Sea. Wine produced for the Roman Empire was aged in caves dug into the Lebanese mountains. The Romans even dedicated a temple in Baalbek to Bacchus, the god of wine.

Today, wine continues to be a major export.

Bhamdoun, one small mountain village known for its ideal climate and soil for growing grapes, is home to more than 52 varieties of vines.

The Lebanese people suffered greatly during seventeen years of war in their small country. Though I am too young to remember those dark days, I know from my parents that no one wins in wartime.

The way forward follows the path of peace. It is a road we must walk together, hand in hand—Fadia, Maroun, Walid, Alia, and all the others. In this way we can truly live in peace, respecting our differences and celebrating the many things we share.

My name, Kareem, means "generous." My sister's name, Amal, means "hope." Our parents always remind us that hope and generosity can change the world.

www.uri.org/kids/world.htm
www.un.org/Pubs/CyberSchoolBus/index.asp

eXpressions

From the moment we wake up each day, our expressive Arabic language offers many opportunities to show affection, appreciation, and goodwill.

Good Morning!
Sabah al Kheir–morning of goodness
Sabah al Nour–morning of light

Upon waking
Sahannawm–healthy sleep

Between loved ones
Habibi–my love, *Aa'yuni*–my eyes, *Albi*–my heart,
Ruhi–my soul, *Hayati*–my life

Meal times
Sallim ideiki–May God keep your hands safe,
Kasak–your glass, *Sahtain*–two healths

Appreciation for hard work
Yaa'tik il aa'fiyeh–God give you health

After bath or haircut
Naa'iman–Heavenly

Birthdays
Aa'bail mit sine–May you reach 100
Il omor killo–all the years to you

Bedtime
Tusbah aa'la kheir–May you greet the morning in goodness

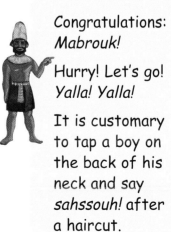

Congratulations: *Mabrouk!*

Hurry! Let's go! *Yalla! Yalla!*

It is customary to tap a boy on the back of his neck and say *sahssouh!* after a haircut.

Yansoon

As in many parts of the world, we in Lebanon use local plants, herbs and some household ingredients to make home **remedies**. The kitchen pantry can quickly double as a medicine chest.

Nothing can replace a visit to the doctor and prescribed medicine when you are very ill, but some of these natural cures really do make us feel better. A few even taste good!

Anise seed (*yansoon*) is infused with water to settle the stomach or soothe a colicky baby.

Mint (*naa'naa*) aids digestion and can also help relieve symptoms at the start of a cold.

Garlic (*toom*) is good for the heart, reduces cholesterol, and can help fight a cold. Press a cut clove of garlic on a bee sting to take away the pain.

Yogurt (*laban*) has live bacteria that are good for the stomach.

Olive oil (*zeit zeitoon*) warm on a cotton ball helps relieve an earache. Olive oil also smoothes skin and makes hair shiny.

Rose water (*mawarid*) is used as an antiseptic for the eyes. When mixed with a little cornstarch and spread on the skin it can help clear a rash or soothe a sunburn.

Orange blossom water (*mazahr*) mixed with hot water aids digestion. It can also be inhaled to revive a person who has fainted.

Instead of chicken soup, children in Lebanon are given rice with plain yogurt when they are unwell.

Zaffé

Boom ba ba boom ba ba boom!

At the sound of the drums, Amal and I scramble to find a place in the crowd near the wide doors of the banquet hall. Bursting through the doors, dancers and musicians in colorful traditional dress part the crowd to make way for the wedding couple. The *zaffé* has begun!

In joyous commotion, drums beat, tambourines jingle and women **trill**, proclaiming blessings on the bride and groom. Torchbearers and swordsmen create an arch with their arms raised. The couple parades through as rose petals rain down on them. Soon everyone is dancing and the festivities begin.

Our alphabetical journey ends with a celebration of love and life. We hope you enjoyed learning about Lebanon—its history, geography, culture and most especially its people.

Maa salemeh!
Au revoir!
Goodbye!

FUN FACTS

Many English words have Arabic roots— algebra, coffee, safari, sugar and zero, to name a few.

123456789 are called Arabic numerals. Arabic speakers use the Hindi numeral system ١٢٣٤٥٦٧٨٩.

Some scholars believe that Phoenician sailors landed in North America around 2,500 years before Christopher Columbus.

Nineteenth-century European travelers Bartlett and Roberts rendered drawings of Lebanon that have become popular prints today.

Lebanon was part of the historic Silk Route.

Paris, France, has its own *Place de Beyrouth*, home to many Lebanese restaurants.

The USA has more than 50 cities and towns named after Lebanon.

Europa, mythical princess of Tyre, is Europe's namesake.

Hermès, an exclusive French design house, commemorated Lebanon with a silk scarf.

Dr. Michael Debakey, world-famous heart surgeon, is a pioneer in the development of the artificial heart.

Mr. Charles Malek, a distinguished Lebanese statesman, co-authored the UN charter with Eleanor Roosevelt.

The intrepid British explorer, Lady Hester Stanhope (1776-1839), dressed as a man in order to assume a leadership role in Lebanon in the early nineteenth century.

COUNTRY FACTS

Capital:	Beirut
Population:	approximately 4 million
Major Cities:	Tripoli, Sidon, Jounieh, Tyre
Land Area:	10,452 sq. km (4,015 sq. miles)
Highest point:	Qurnat as Sawda - 3,083 meters (10,115 feet)
Coastline:	210 km (131 miles)
Major Rivers:	Litani, Hasbani, Assi
Major Religions:	Christianity, Druze and Islam
National Anthem:	*Kulloona lil Watan* (All together for the country)
Independence Day:	November 22
Form of Government:	Republic and Parliamentary Democracy
Economy:	Free market, based on tourism and services
Currency:	Lebanese lira and US dollar
Wildlife:	Fox, bats, badgers, migratory birds

GLOSSARY

agora: a gathering place or marketplace. Merchants at the agora in ancient Tyre sold everything from food to precious jewelry.

ancestor: a person from whom one is descended. My ancestors came to Australia from Lebanon about one hundred years ago.

aqueduct: a channel or pipe built to carry water over a long distance. Aqueducts use gravity to direct water across great distances.

archeologist: a person who studies past human life. Archeologists from Germany, France and America work with Lebanese archeologists to learn more about early settlers in the region.

diversity: made up of different kinds or sorts. Eighteen religious communities create a natural diversity in Lebanon.

emigrate: to leave one country or region in order to settle in another. Many Lebanese emigrate to live in France.

Epiphany: January 6th, the traditional day the Magi, or kings, arrived to see the newborn Jesus. It is customary to eat a special cake with a bean hidden in it on Epiphany. The person who gets the bean is "king."

famine: a great lack of food over a wide area. Famine forced many Lebanese to leave their country in the nineteenth century.

folkloric: traditional customs, clothing, music, dance, stories, and art preserved among a people. Much of Lebanon's folkloric music describes village life.

inaugural: relating to the official ceremony which marks the beginning of a presidential term. Lebanon's president is inaugurated into office every six years.

minaret: a tall slender tower of a mosque having one or more balconies from which the summons to prayer is called by the mue'zzin. In Beirut, minarets and church steeples dapple the skyline.

necropolis: a cemetery or burial site. Necropolis is a Greek word which literally means "city of the dead."

Ottoman: relating to the Turkish Empire. The Ottoman Empire ruled the Middle East, Greece, Asia Minor and the Balkans for 400 years.

Phoenician: Semitic people who established city-states in what is now known as Lebanon. Phoenician sailors were skilled navigators capable of traveling long distances.

Ramadan: the ninth month of the Muslim lunar calendar. During the holy month of Ramadan, Muslims fast from dawn until dusk.

remedy: something used to take away pain or heal a disease. My grandmother claims that laughter is the best remedy.

resin: a sticky substance produced by fir trees and certain other plants. Resin is used to make plastics, medicines, paints and other products.

spelunker: explorers who measure and map caves. Spelunkers report on plants and animals found in caves.

stalactite: a rock formation that looks like an icicle and hangs from the roof of a cave. There is a stalactite in the Jeita Grotto which measures more than eight meters.

stalagmite: a rock formation that looks like a cone and is built upwards from the floor of a cave. Stalagmites are formed by the minerals in dripping water.

trill: a trembling or quivering sound made by a singing voice or musical instruments. Village women trill to announce the bride at weddings.

INDEX

AUTHORS

MARIJEAN MORAN BOUERI was born in Philadelpia. After studying English Literature and Art History at St. Mary's College, Notre Dame, Indiana, she had many diverse experiences from researching rare manuscripts to designing men's sportswear. Marijean and her husband, François, along with their three children, have lived in Amsterdam, Brussels, and finally Beirut. Marijean, author of *Lebanon 1-2-3: A Counting Book in Three Languages*, is a passionate collector of children's books.

JILL JOHNSON BOUTROS grew up in Minnesota, knowing one day she would see the world. With a bachelor's degree from Notre Dame and a master's in education from Columbia University, she set off to teach in New York, New Jersey and finally in London. In 1999, she and her husband, Naji, moved their family to his childhood village in Lebanon. The following year they founded Château Belle-Vue vineyards, employing local people and encouraging the community to tend the valley once more. Jill and Naji live in a traditional, red-roofed Lebanese mountain home with their four children, Philippe, Hannah, Lauren and Ella... along with sixteen chickens, numerous cats, and a very nervous dog.

A native New Yorker of Greek lineage, JOANNE KERATSOS SAYAD graduated from Marymount Manhattan College with a bachelor's degree in Liberal Arts. She worked at Sotheby's before moving to Beirut in 1991 with her husband, Ralph. They have three children and reside in the Sayad building along with 20 members of their extended family–a modern day tribe! At the American University of Beirut's Archeological Museum, Joanne helped develop cultural workshops for children ages 7-13 and has written a series of articles exploring Lebanon's heritage.

ARTIST

TATIANNA BOTCHAROVA SABBAGH was born in Krasnodar, Russia. After completing her studies at The Art School for Children and Youth, she earned a BA in linguistics from Kuban State University. Tatiana speaks Russian, Italian, French, Arabic and English.

Living in Lebanon since 1996, Sabbagh explores creativity in different forms: she crafts puppets for "Les Amis des Marionettes," teaches children's art classes and prepares art projects for the children's program at the American University of Beirut's Archeological Museum.

Tatiana and her husband, Bassam, have two boys, Alessandro and Giovanni. Amazingly, she still finds time to relax with Tai Chi.